THROUGH
THEIR EYES

POINTS OF VIEW

Edited By Sarah Waterhouse

First published in Great Britain in 2020 by:

Young Writers
Remus House
Coltsfoot Drive
Peterborough
PE2 9BF
Telephone: 01733 890066
Website: www.youngwriters.co.uk

Printed and bound in the UK by BookPrintingUK
Website: www.bookprinting.co.uk
YB0433R

FOREWORD

Since 1991, here at Young Writers we have celebrated the awesome power of creative writing, especially in young adults, where it can serve as a vital method of expressing strong (and sometimes difficult) emotions, a conduit to develop empathy, and a safe, non-judgemental place to explore one's own place in the world. With every poem we see the effort and thought that each pupil published in this book has put into their work and by creating this anthology we hope to encourage them further with the ultimate goal of sparking a life-long love of writing.

Through Their Eyes challenged young writers to open their minds and pen bold, powerful poems from the points-of-view of any person or concept they could imagine – from celebrities and politicians to animals and inanimate objects, or even just to give us a glimpse of the world as they experience it. The result is this fierce collection of poetry that by turns questions injustice, imagines the innermost thoughts of influential figures or simply has fun.

The nature of the topic means that contentious or controversial figures may have been chosen as the narrators, and as such some poems may contain views or thoughts that, although may represent those of the person being written about, by no means reflect the opinions or feelings of either the author or us here at Young Writers.

We encourage young writers to express themselves and address subjects that matter to them, which sometimes means writing about sensitive or difficult topics. If you have been affected by any issues raised in this book, details on where to find help can be found at *www.youngwriters.co.uk/info/other/contact-lines*

CONTENTS

Oliver Kinsman (14)	79
George Collis (11) & Samuel	80
Barbara Skorczak (11), Lily & Francesca	81
Amaya Du Preez (11)	82
Victor Tocca (15)	83

Prenton High School For Girls, Rock Ferry

Alisha Lea (14)	84
Alex Hampson (14)	86
Ellie Oates (14)	88
Lucy Call (14)	90
Chloe Stormont (14)	91
Kai Maclean (14)	92
Angel Elizabeth Brothers (14)	93
Alex Roberts (13)	94
Sheila Negmadin (13)	95

Stokesley School, Stokesley

Nieve Barr (13)	96
Molly Butterfield	99
William Firman (13)	100
Emily Rhodes (13)	102
Polly Hunter (13)	103
Hana Jones (13)	104
Amy Lewis (12)	106
Gabriella Mathers (13)	107
Grace Eve Roberts (13)	108
Leon Moody (13)	110
Bethany Hill (13)	111
Jack Doyle (13)	112
Harley Norton-Moore (14)	113
Alex Bone (13)	114
Edward Lambert (13)	115

Tamworth Enterprise College, Belgrave

Libby Attwood (11)	116
Charlie Winyard (11)	119
Rose Giles (14)	120

Keira Vallery O'Connell (13)	122
Erin Royston (11)	124
Bobby Hickey (11)	126
Ethan Winfield (13)	128
Kiera Elisabeth Bate (12)	130
Jaimeelei Bridgwater (12)	132
Ethan Rowe (11)	134
Skye Ward (11)	135
Evie Alice Ames (11)	136
Hollie Dixon (15)	138
Imogen Daws (11)	140
Alexandra Leskiewicz (12)	142
Kara Thompson (14)	144
Aidan Matthew Whetton (14)	145
Laura Jade McKeown (12)	146
Leland Cooper (12)	148
Maison Biddle (11)	149
Summer Mae McLaren (11)	150
Logan Darson Bennett (12)	151
Stacy Stroud (11)	152
Jessica Jones (11)	153
Luca Sidoli (11)	154
Emma Greenway (12)	155
Shaun David Dunham (12)	156
Ellie-Mae Williams-Moore (11)	157
Oliver Smallwood (11)	158
Oliver Deakin	159
Stella-Faith Powell (14)	160
Lacey Louise Wayne (11)	161
Tia Williams (11)	162
Michael Reeves (12)	163
Amelia Powell (11)	164
Jake Inscoe (12)	165
Charlie Arthur Taylor (11)	166
Rivith Weligama Palliyaguruge (11)	167
Flynn Francis (11)	168
Alaric James Johnson (11)	169
Max David Wiseman (15)	170
McKenzie Lowe (14)	171
Jack Stephen Mott (12)	172
Lily-May Deakin (12)	173
James Malin (11)	174
Owen Mudie (11)	175

THE
POEMS

The Soldiers Of War

Caged within an encircling wire, heart, soul and mind afire,
Fighting soldiers from the sky, fearless men who jump and die,
The dying night was broken by a single ray of hope,
Shone fiercest on this, my darkest day,
Waves of anger and fear circulate over the bright,
Uncertain and afraid, visions of comrades sharing a fight,
While there was a raid.

They walked miles on foot,
Losing loved ones on the way,
Through grim dirt and soot, travelling night and day.
Many young men have died here, sacrifices were made.
But was it worth it? Did it bring any change?
A family of soldiers walking shoulder and shoulder.
The world you are carrying just like a boulder.

The tears come down and down.
But you don't try, like men do, to stop them now.
How much could you bear or even dream to think what it's like out here as me?
People say it's the best to die in this way,
But you know all too well that there are better ways,
He's just another soldier out of millions dying that you should see.

A nightmare, but wake up, boy,
This is reality.

Matilde Henriques Niza (12)
Blessed William Howard Catholic High School, Stafford

The Day Was Cold

The day was cold
It was always cold
Even though I was told
It was summer,
It didn't feel like summer.
I didn't feel good
I got out of prison that day
I have been in prison for four years
I haven't seen my two little girls in four years
They are now eight
I wonder how they are
My mum was driving me home
A cold shiver ran down my neck
I was worried...

I got out the car
My two little girls came running to me
I ran into the house
I saw my dog sat on my favourite chair
I got into the shower to wash my hair
I heard a strange laughter
That didn't sound like anyone in the house when I walked in.
I got out of the shower
Seeing someone watching me
I was worried...

I got into my pyjamas
I heard the laughter again
I looked around and saw nothing
I tried to get to sleep
I couldn't stop thinking about it
I finally got to sleep...

In the morning I looked at my phone
I got a video message
I pressed play,
It was a video that said a girl died the day she got out of prison.
When she got out of her mum's car
She fell in a sewer hole on her street
Her neck was broken
Her face was torn off
Her name was Katie Manely
She died today at 2.30pm.
It was 3.30pm
I looked up and screamed...

Was I a ghost?
No, I couldn't be!
I saw my mum and dad crying
I looked in the mirror
I was gone forever...

Ruby Woolley (11)
Blessed William Howard Catholic High School, Stafford

Running Free

I am a dolphin swimming free,
Splashing in the waves and swimming in the sea.
Chuckling children surfing in the sea,
I swim and swim but they don't see me.
Then they see me and they say, "Arw!"
Arw? That's all you have?
It should be, "Wow! Look, a dolphin!"

I am a monkey swinging in the trees,
Jumping from tree to tree is all I do,
Except eating, sleeping and running free,
Sometimes I see people and they feed me.
I grow up in a place
But I don't know where I am.
At first, I thought I was in the Amazon rainforest or an
English wood
But then my mum told me
I live in a... zoo!

I am a leopard cub running free,
Chasing my sisters and fighting my brothers.
One day, I saw a panther
It chased me back to my den
Then I realised it wanted to play again.
My mum warned me about panther games,
She said they were rough.

I wanted to play but my mum said I had to be tough.

The next day, I had so much energy but no one would play.
So I found a monkey, but it slapped me so I got mad.
I bit it!
Then it fell over, I think it died!
I took it back to my den with a lot of pride.
My dad was so proud,
My mum just frowned,
But then they started to eat it!
I got confused so I ran away,
That's why I'm here today.
Running free!

Bethan Eyton-Jones (11)
Blessed William Howard Catholic High School, Stafford

Is It Worth It?

Is it worth coming home in fear to go out again,
To feel trapped in your own body,
To feel like everyone around you laughs at your very
appearance,
Is it worth it?

Is it worth changing who you are
Because your 'friends' don't like the way you look or even
talk,
Or staring at yourself in the mirror,
Wondering why you look the way you look,
Is it worth it?

Is it worth screaming at your parents
Because they give you advice that you don't like,
Or maybe shouting at someone because they made a tiny
mistake,
Such as saying one plus one is three,
Is it worth it?

Is it worth pulling yourself out of doing something because
it's not 'cool',
Or not doing what you love because other people don't like
it,
Is it worth it?

Is it worth flunking out of school because you don't get the
grade you want,
Or sitting next to somebody you don't like,

Is it worth it?

Is it worth running up to your bedroom,
Hiding under your covers,
Refusing to come out because you got bullied or picked on,
Is it worth it?

No.
No, it's not.
It's worth doing what you love because you love it,
And standing up to the people who don't like you.
You're perfect in your own way.
That's worth it.

Evanne Jessica Birkett (11)
Blessed William Howard Catholic High School, Stafford

A Rose In Flames

You'd think my life is simple
I'm beautiful
I'm angelic
I'm perfect
I wish it was different

People glaring, staring,
"Oh, how exquisite!"
Only admiring my outside,
Not caring about my broken inside.

My beauty is pain,
As I hear voices
Deafening me.
As I scream in terror,
A silent scream
And sob in secret.

My thorns
Cutting my inside,
Revealing blood,
Tearing my self-esteem
As my confidence dies
A slow, painful death.

My petals fall and shrivel as few remain
Little stay healthy
Yet still, I'm beautiful

Yet still, I feel pain.

Nobody will take
Any opportunity
To see themselves
Through my eyes
As I am just
A stick with a pretty bud
No purpose
No feelings
Do I matter?

As my self-esteem dies,
My petals fall
And shrivel
As I ask myself, "Why?"
I would say
I was misunderstood,
But I...
I don't matter.

As my last petal falls,
I shed a final tear,
As all hope is lost
And my 'perfect' life's end
Is near.
I shrivel like a stick
With a blood-red soul,
As my depression puts me,

A once beautiful rose,
In red, vicious flames.

Chloe Harris (11)
Blessed William Howard Catholic High School, Stafford

Blood Surrounds Me

B y the time I woke up, my hands were covered in blood again,
L ike the time he made me kill my family,
O n the field I was, the trees glaring at me,
O n the field by the house that my family were killed in,
D eath encloses me now, it feels easiest to yield to it.

C an't I just live a normal life as a normal teen,
O r without my boyfriend?
V ery abusive he is, and manipulative,
E verything he makes me do stays with me,
R ight now, all I can hear are the screams of those killed,
I am to blame for all those killed,
N ow I wish I could stand up to him,
G one are all those I knew and loved.

L ove now feels like a pitiful thing for me,
I wish I had never met him,
F utile is everything I could do,
E verything I think leads back to him.

Iona Adamson (11)
Blessed William Howard Catholic High School, Stafford

The Corpse

A room.
A bed.
A myriad of faces.
I am dead.
They cry, they mourn,
They laugh, they scorn.
Now I have passed,
They all blurt my faults; at last.

Time flies by, a church, goodbyes;
A priest and now the sky.
Out in the wind, with the gulls,
I can see my son strain as he pulls
My coffin.

Dirt. It rains down into my grave from above.
A man with a shovel, standing in the mud.

Black. My vision is dead.
I can smell my stomach as the maggots devour.
(I smell awful - I must take a shower!)
I try to move my arm, but... no.
I died long ago.

This is the end.
I am dead.
Now send the angels from the land of above,
A spirit or maybe a dove.

I wait for days...

Oh please, let this end!
Oh please, my heart needs to mend!
But no angels shall come, no spirit, no dove
Or sign from above.
I lay here, a corpse,
With no hope of return to the land above the soil,
Waiting like Satan's rotting royal.

Death was my final wish: foolish!
Oh please, let me live!
I treated life with no care when I was a kid.
Wasted time, wasted life.
So if you really are up there,
Please slit my soul with your scythe.

Let me die.

Felix Bance (11)

Blessed William Howard Catholic High School, Stafford

The Lonely Tree

Here I stand,
While upon the hill,
The sun's coming up,
What a big deal.

It passes overhead
And the day is done,
I am so bored,
I had no fun.

The next day comes,
Same old, same old,
Till what do I see?
A boy with eyes of gold.

He trots over the hill
And to my surprise,
The boy has a friend,
Wait... is that a pie?

Oh, I can't wait
Until they come,
They must climb on my trunk,
It is such fun.

Finally, they arrive
And put the pie down,
They then high-fived
And ran around on the ground.

One climbed first,
Then the second one came,
Up they went,
Higher than a plane.

Hours went by
And the sun started to drop,
Both jumped out of my hair,
The pie was soon gone.

The boys had a laugh,
Then high-fived once more,
They began trotting down the hill,
Why? What have I done?

I understood,
The sun was coming down,
But one more minute,
Please turn around.

Soon they were out of sight
And I was alone,
I had so much fun, though
I began to moan.

Thinking back on it,
It was an amazing time,
I hope they come again,
Wouldn't trade it for a dime.

Arun White (12)

Blessed William Howard Catholic High School, Stafford

Do You Remember Me?

I used to be loved and hugged all the time,
But now I pass the time with the odd rhyme,
I used to go everywhere with you,
Although it sometimes annoyed me when you always
watched Elf.
But now I'd give anything to watch it with you,
Because now I'm just stuck on a shelf.
The bedroom I was in when you went to school was cool
and airy,
But now, in the charity shop, it's hot and stuffy and a tiny bit
scary.
When I was with you, I knew I was loved,
But now I'm at the back of the shelf, shoved, unloved.
Do you remember me?
I hope you do.

What happened to me?
What did I do?
Is it because you grew up?
Did you grow out of me too?
Do you remember me?
I hope you do.

You used to love me,
What came over you?
I hope you regret this,
I truly hope you do.

Do you remember me?
I hope you do.

You have a family,
Like I used to,
You still have yours,
But mine was you.
Do you remember me?
I hope you do.

Leah Strickland (11)
Blessed William Howard Catholic High School, Stafford

Access Denied...

Stayin' in all day,
Always hackin' the same old way.
Hiding in the dark, in plain sight,
Only seen in the dead of night.
Mess with me, say goodbye
To your lives, work and an extra surprise...

You never know when I'll attack,
Let alone where with my access hack.
I destroy mainframes with my malware,
Take your money and a little jumpscare!

I use my worm, they always miss 'em,
Sentient a virus, annihilating your system.
Then again, I'm not that bad,
Sometimes I help those who are sad,
By taking their computer and sellin' it for scrap.
All this crime soon put me on the map.

And all this time and determination
Served on my own guide.
With time on my side,
Consequences, they increase,
Every time that I seize.

Every new account
Always ups the malware count.
My only hope and dream:

To control the data stream.
"Hey! Do you understand me?"
"Uh, later! Absolute loser."

Phillip Waltho (11)

Blessed William Howard Catholic High School, Stafford

Past...

Have you ever stepped inside someone else's shoes
And that someone was a some*thing*?
Maybe that something has felt its big purpose was on the loose
And maybe that something has something to do with you.

An old drawing or photograph,
Something from your childhood,
Something from your past,
Well, what if I told you I could do all that?

Tell you their feelings,
Just like poor me,
I'm a drawing,
A lonely one, you see.

I'm from a kid's past,
A kid who is great,
A kid with much better art abilities
Than when they were eight!

This is me,
An old drawing, you see,
With three fingers on each skinny palm,
A nose, legs and a chubby tummy.

I have so many flaws but someone once told me
Looks don't matter,

It's you, yourself and we
Who can see your inner beauty.

Laila Temple (11)
Blessed William Howard Catholic High School, Stafford

Paramedic Call-Out

Sitting in my office,
Waiting to be called,
I've got to keep my patience,
There is a call.
I dived out of my seat
In a rush to the phone,
I answered.

I got called to go
And check on someone
Who was having a mimic stroke,
She was ten years of age.

I was thinking,
*Why is this happening
To a ten-year-old?*

I jumped into the driver's seat,
Put the lights on and started to drive.

I pulled up at the house,
Got out of the ambulance,
Got my stuff ready and
Walked around the side of the ambulance,
Then walked towards the door.

I had nerves until I got to the door,
That's when there was awkward silence.

After seconds, there was me knocking on the door,
I entered and there was Kaci lying on the sofa...

Kaci Mathers (12)
Blessed William Howard Catholic High School, Stafford

How I Wish For A Nice Warm Home

I'm a depressed pencil that is treated with *no* respect,
Every day is different but the same.
I don't know what to expect!
All the time I wish no one ever came.
How I wish for a nice warm home.

I feel like a boomerang,
Thrown from side to side.
When I am dropped, I hear a huge bang!
Stupidly, they sometimes make me a slide.
How I wish for a nice warm home.

Oh, and as well as being thrown,
I am *always* chewed down to the bone!
I'm spun and spun and spun,
Yet they never take me for a run.
How I wish for a nice warm home.

Overall, my worst fear is being sucked,
A holiday is what I need to have booked!
Every day I'm sharpened, I'm getting shorter and shorter,
My length has already been reduced by a quarter!
Oh, how I wish for a nice warm home.

Lily Cochrane (11)
Blessed William Howard Catholic High School, Stafford

The Life Of A Dodo

As I bounce and bounce
All I can think of is, *I need food! I need food!*
But when I see a hunter
All I can say is, "I don't want blood! I don't want blood!"
As I grow up, I try to survive
But everywhere I go, there's always a hunter that follows.
All I want is food and water,
But as I travel through the forests, it just gets hotter.
I'm now endangered
There are only ten of my kind left.
We have to find a meeting spot but the other hunters have
done theft.
Now there's just me, but after me, there's nothing,
I'm getting older now and I keep coughing,
Finally, a hunter catches me
As the killer spear gets through my back
My knee is in a lock
And now I'm dead,
On my death bed,
But at least I found food and lived out my life.

Wesley Emile Nelson (11)
Blessed William Howard Catholic High School, Stafford

Reach For The Stars

Jump and balance, dancing in space,
I have strength and pure grace.
Dedication to the heart and you will
Have long hours of practise to develop the skill.

On the bars or beam, vault or the floor,
Everyone cheers but it comes down to the score.
Each movement we fear precision and then
Stick the landing, it's a perfect ten!

You feel the loss and pain and defeat,
But still are able to stand on two feet.
I never give up, I am always strong,
This is what I have been training for all along.

I jump off the beam, flip off the bars,
I follow my dreams and reach for the stars.
Live your life and risk it all,
Take some chances, take the fall.
Take your time, no need to hurry,
Have some fun and never worry.
I am a gymnast!

Grace Taylor (11)
Blessed William Howard Catholic High School, Stafford

Why?

My first day at high school,
Ready to learn,
Palms so sweaty,
Feel like I'm going to burn.
Lots of things on my mind,
But why this?
There is a girl pushing and shoving me,
Another thing added to my worry list.
I'm being whirled around and called names,
Please stop,
You're being a pain.
Each day this happens and I wonder why,
Some days I want to die.
But someone told me that's not right,
Told the teacher,
We were talking all night.
The next morning, it was fine,
I felt like I had finished a huge climb,
So don't do what I did,
It's not okay,
Live your life and have happy days!

Annabelle Wootton (11)
Blessed William Howard Catholic High School, Stafford

If Only...

Simple. Plain. Too blank.
Nothing. Nothingness. Bored.
I wish I could see the world.
I wish I could draw my feelings.
If only I could...
Nobody understands.

Life. Does it matter?
If only I did...
I need the answer!
I'm tired of waiting for years.
It just brings me to tears.
Wow, I just rhymed!
But why would that help?

What is the point? Why?
Why am I here? Why?
Why does life even exist?
Why?

Sometimes I just think...
If only...
Could I make a change?

Too many questions to ask.
Too little time.
If only I had more...

Have you guessed yet? No?
I'm the pencil and this is the story of my life!

Emily Neupauer (12)

Blessed William Howard Catholic High School, Stafford

I'm Still Me

Snapped and scraped and scarred
Is what I'll always be.
Doodled and taped and carved,
But I'm still me.

I'm used for a great load of writing,
Okay, I'm a tiny bit wee.
Who cares what I've been through?
Because I'm still me!

I've been mistaken for a biscuit,
I've even been dunked in tea.
It tasted nice and sweet, and look:
I'm still me.

No matter about all of my scratches,
My flaws that make them all flee.
I won't hide my differences,
Yeah, I'm still me!

Whenever you feel lousy,
Or as useful as a flea,
Stand out and be unique
And shout: "I'm still me!"

Saoirse Boydon (11)
Blessed William Howard Catholic High School, Stafford

Boris' Prime Time

The news was true
Theresa May has been fired
I could finally get the job
I've always admired

It's not been easy
It's been hard every day
As Jeremy Corbyn
Has tried to ruin the day.

On the 31st of October
I'll get the job done
Oh my!
This will be fun

You can cry if you must
But this time
It will be Jeremy Corbyn
Who's laying in the dust

Some MPs said
I'm making a mistake
But getting Brexit done
Is a piece of cake

So goodbye Europe
You'll finally see
The reason it all happened
Was because of me.

Harry James Smith (11)
Blessed William Howard Catholic High School, Stafford

Prisoner Of War

That night felt like years,
Quiet rumbling in the distance,
With people screaming outside.

I could never forget the soldier's face
As he grabbed me and flung me over his shoulder,
I kicked and screamed
But all he did was chuck me in the prison.

I cried with fear and anger,
The other children stayed quiet like they got threatened,
But I didn't care,
I wanted to go home...

Bombs dropped and people shook,
Those twelve hours felt like an eternity.
I eventually fell asleep and woke up,
It was just another nightmare from last year...

Yasmin Desoky (12)
Blessed William Howard Catholic High School, Stafford

What Am I?

It's hectic where I am,
Teens screaming and shouting,
Children laughing and crying,
There are rules where I am,
But not like the law,
There are pens and pencils here,
Fights and rights also
And when everybody's gone,
Out go all the lights,
Then I am calm and still,
Ready to rest,
But when dawn comes
And the clock hits nine,
Everybody's back!
Everybody's again on my land,
But this is where I stand
(I can't move).
I am education,
I am a tool
You've probably guessed it now,
But I am
A great big...
School!

Oliver Bishop (12)
Blessed William Howard Catholic High School, Stafford

Wild Tiger

Bang!

They have found me.
What would I do?
Where would I go?

I've hidden for years,
I've hunted little.
Do they not get it?
I want to live!
I want to be free!

I dart through the forest,
The trees stare at me with sad eyes as I run.

I can't lash out!
They'll definitely kill me then!
But would that be better than running forever?

Are they still behind me?
No! They're not!
I need to find somewhere to stay

Until next time...

Emilia Victoria Coombs-Fielding (12)
Blessed William Howard Catholic High School, Stafford

This Is To Megan And Her Feelings

It's hard when you feel like no one loves you
Because you like girls or you're transgender
And they make fun of you
But what I have learned about life
Is not what *they* think
It's what *you* think
Because God made you unique
It's not the outside that counts
It's the inside that counts the most
So be you because you can be no one else!
Keep being you and shine like the diamond you are
Shine bright
Because you are loved by more people than you think
So remember that.

Elle Insull (12)

Blessed William Howard Catholic High School, Stafford

A Lost Kitten

I sat at the door
Wondering what's out there
Will I get out
Or will I stay in
Sat down by the bin?

Then the door opened
I wondered by who
Then I saw
My owner out there
Behind me, eating a pear

I stepped outside
Slowly and cautiously
I rolled on the grass
I wandered too far
I turned back, there was no door

Where should I go?
I wondered whether to leave
Try to find home
I turned around
And started to bound.

Isobel Furber (11)
Blessed William Howard Catholic High School, Stafford

A Story Of The Past

That long and terrible night,
The sound we all feared -
The air raid sirens,
Distant rumbling,
Roars of approaching bombers;

No words could speak our horror,
No tears could cry our sorrow.
Away from the city, I watched,
Shivering;

What a terrible thing it was -
Thousands of people, trapped.
We left the city to burn
And went on;

I remember that night well,
It makes me ashamed
To tell you
And I want you to know
That I would have wished to turn away.

Ruby Chapman-Murphy (11) & Harley
Blessed William Howard Catholic High School, Stafford

Memory Field

Working in the field
Was like running through the past,
I didn't run slow
But also not fast.

I knew my family loved me,
I was that kind of dog,
Although they did get annoyed
When I'd bring in a log.

I watched my family's daughter,
On the slide she played,
But she couldn't get down
When at the bottom there I laid.

I knew we wouldn't stay together
Because no one lives forever,
But as long as I'm here,
I won't shed a tear.

Amy Trickett (11)
Blessed William Howard Catholic High School, Stafford

The Mirror

On the day that I was bought
I was happy, or so I thought
Tightly wrapped
Happy but flat
After that
My life went *splat!*

This and that
Every second
Every minute
Every hour
Every day
Every month

She would twist
And turn
Smile
And laugh
Could I just crack?

I would copy her every move
It was the same every day
Make-up, hair, costume, practise

Can I just crack?

Melissa Simpson (11)
Blessed William Howard Catholic High School, Stafford

You

It's hard when people come up to you
And laugh at you and bully you
Like if you're a girl but you like boy things
Or you're a boy who likes girl things
But that doesn't make it right for people to be mean,
horrible and bully you.
It is like sitting in a cupboard, locked away,
Letting the world forget you existed.
No one should ever bully you,
Just remember, there is one of you
And you only have one life
So you should be able to enjoy it.

Georgia Smith (11)
Blessed William Howard Catholic High School, Stafford

A Football's Life

Being a football can be very fun
Especially when I'm kicked faster than the players can run.
Although I feel sorry when they play in the rain
And I hit the players and cause a stinging pain.
This is very sad
Being a football can be bad.

All day long, I'm kicked around
On the wet and soggy ground.
Sometimes I'm flat,
Then look quite fat.

After all,
I'm just a ball!

Joshua Hyden (11)
Blessed William Howard Catholic High School, Stafford

I Call, I Squeak, I Plead

You find me in a shop,
You clean me
You sit, sit, sit on me,
I call, I squeak, I plead,
"Oh please let me watch the TV!"
I call, I squeak, I plead.
I hear the remote laughing,
I hear the tea mugs cheering,
I hear the table crying,
I call, I squeak, I plead,
"Oh why, oh why do you block my vision?"
I call,
I squeak,
I plead.

Darcy Boydon (11)
Blessed William Howard Catholic High School, Stafford

Dog's Life

Cute little dogs
Running around in fog.

They lick bones
LIke we like to lick ice cream cones.

They don't watch TV like us
Or shop with us.

They sleep all day
Like peaceful angels.

At night, they can't close their eyes,
Making sure that we are alright.

Vilte Poskute (11)
Blessed William Howard Catholic High School, Stafford

The Painting On The Wall

I stay on the shelf, never to be touched.
I stay in the gallery to look nice.
Nobody ever appreciates
The real me inside
Behind all the paint and ink
Behind all the bright colours.
Maybe if you looked closer
Maybe if you really think
Then you would see
The real me.

Xanthe Banham (11)
Blessed William Howard Catholic High School, Stafford

The Dodo

Bang!
Bang!

What have I done?
What have I done to make them so angry
So violent?
I'm just a bird
Without any friends or family
I'm just alone
A lonely dodo
With nothing

Click click
Bang!
Extinct!

James Condron (11)
Blessed William Howard Catholic High School, Stafford

I'm Different

J ealous of people who don't get judged
A time when I wasn't gay I was liked.
M akes me feel like I don't deserve to live.
E veryone hates me.
S ituations can get physical.

Adam Jaromin (11)
Blessed William Howard Catholic High School, Stafford

The Siberian Tiger In The Circus

We don't perform because we want to,
We perform because we are afraid not to.
We don't go outside because we don't want to,
We don't go outside because we're not allowed to.
We don't fight because we want to,
We fight because we are forced to.

It's time to perform and jump through hoops of fire that burn my skin.
Children clap and adults cheer, my ears are bleeding make it stop.
Back to the cage of horrors I go for it to all start again tomorrow.

Oh, how I wish to be free and know what it feels like to be wild
And to do what a tiger should do.
Oh, how I wish to have a family who loves me for me.
But my biggest wish of all is to teach my cubs to hunt.

Scarlett River Gilbert (12)

Chelsea Academy, London

The War Of Lies

When I was a lad,
I had a future and a wife,
Life was good but times were bad,
Full of constant strife,
Ol' Churchill had our wages cut,
As Hitler marched forward,
The mournful cries of my gut,
But yet I marched onward.

I marched up the road ahead,
My khaki uniform clean,
A steel helmet adorned my head,
Surrounded by all this green,
The sun shone on my knife,
My bayonet by my side,
Both I use to take a life,
Or I will die.

My shovel dug into the dirt,
My face flecked with sweat,
Scrapes and cuts, they really hurt,
As the shovel and earth met,
A hole for a home is all we had,
And a bed of soil and mud,
The constant digging driving me mad,
Prey to rats and bugs.

Night came so I said my prayers,

The bombs kept me up,
The whistling of bullets cutting the air,
And the bang of a gun,
The rain came,
The tears of God,
The soldier's bane,
Mixed with sod,
This was hell's domain,
The mule's gentle plod.

The sergeant's whistle woke me up,
It was Death's call,
Only fools and those with luck,
Would go up there at all,
Death in hell was the share,
Of those who walked the Devil's place,
Blood and tears were the fare,
Nowhere was safe.

I dashed across the desolate land,
As I let out a sigh,
My gun and knife in my hand,
A bullet struck my thigh,
I limped on in agony,
Death awaited me on both sides,
So then I realised sadly this war was a lie.

No spoils for the soldiers,
No glory for the winners,

No spine between your shoulders,
Just a world of sinners,
Hate between brethren,
Countless deaths at a time,
Betrayal between friends,
That's the war for which I signed.

I limped forward past the pain,
My comrades in tow,
The bombs and missiles fell like rain,
Blood soaked the snow,
The machine gun peppered our ranks,
The bodies piled up high,
Far away a column of tanks,
We all will die.

My bayonet raised,
My life resigned,
Our spirits razed,
I lost my mind,
I charged the enemy from the right,
My blood dripped,
I let out a cry,
O' world, goodbye.

Sisay Michael Tegegne (12)
Chelsea Academy, London

You See...

You see the sun,
Here comes the rain,
Forget your kite?
It's lost again.

You're a bee,
You see a flower,
you see a light,
it's your last shower.

You're a moth,
You see a cave,
You see a light,
You meet your grave.

You're a fox,
You hide in a shed,
You see a girl,
Her rake makes you dead.

You're a snowman,
The rain has fallen,
You had a smile,
But now it's gone.

You're a human,
You see another,
If she gives you a smile,
Go run for cover!

Amelie Reeve (14)
Chelsea Academy, London

T'e Aitc' Dropped Off My Keyboard!

T'e aitc' dropped off my keyboard
I t'ink it must be fate
Because t'e Englis' drop t'eir aitc'es
It's a well-known accent trait.

T'e aitc' dropped off my keyboard
I don't know w'ere it went
Per'aps it rolled off to 'amps'ire
'ertfords'ire or maybe even Kent.

T'e aitc' dropped off my keyboard
I wis' t'at it would mend
For now, I drop my aitc'es
At t'e beginning, middle and end!

But w'en you write your letters
T'ere's no aitc' w'ere it oug't to appear,
T'ough elocution won't be necessary
T'ere won't be an aitc' for you to 'ear.

So 'ere, let me explain my point
For 'er majesty, t'e Queen
Don't say 'aitch but Aitch, you see,
So maybe t'is problem's not so mean.

I've been taught not to drop my 'aitc'es
I'm sorry my 'onoured William Blake
But t'e 'aitch you all speak of, well,
Never started wit' an I-I !!

T'ere may be a 'ole in my keyboard,
And it's no longer fit pretend
But it won't stop me typing
I'll be a writer till t'e end.

Monty Pratt
Chelsea Academy, London

Breakfast At Tiffany's

As usual, she walked down the street looking wise,
But a man called out whom she did not recognize.

Past him, up the building she hurried,
But he was fast and caught up, banging on the door saying
his feelings were buried.

Later, the buzz sounded and Ms Holly's cat was not too
pleased,
And neither was Ms Holly when he came to let her know.

She got up, feeling low from the tiredness, letting the
unknown buzzer in; From the door was Ms Holly Golightly's
head peeking.

After a little while, a Mr Paul was leaning against her door,
Ms Holly was quite in awe for she had never seen such a
man in the building. She paused.

He asked to use the phone, but it was no use,
Ms Holly's ears, from silence, were ringing, her earplugs
were infused in.

Eventually, Ms Holly understood that Mr Paul needed to call
the next of kin.

She let him in, opened the fridge door to find a shoe,
Ms Holly did not care but could not help being confused.

Mr Paul stopped what he was doing, amused.
And oh! This is where a story of love and tragedy and drama starts,
Right here, right now, even though neither of them knew
That they would just stick like glue.

Scarlett Brazy (12)
Chelsea Academy, London

Angel

Dear Angel, oh Angel
Guide me through
All the time I spend with you
Help me to know
What I may do for you

Dear Angel, oh Angel
You make me have pleasure
I know that for sure

I feel kind, warm and cosy with you
Keep me safe under your wing

Dear Angel, oh Angel
Without you I'm sad
If I look up in the sky
I'll see you
And believe I'm with you!

Nikol Aleksieieva (12)
Chelsea Academy, London

It's Coming From That Box

What's that smell? That fresh, clean, soapy essence...
It's coming from that box.

What's that noise? Scratching, scraping, sniffing...
It's coming from that box.

What's that taste? Sweet, scrumptious-smelling something
which makes me drool...
It's coming from that box.

What's that I see? It wiggles from side to side...
It's coming from that box.

What's that I feel? It's like a radiator, all warmth...
It's coming from that box.

What even is this? Sapphire-blue eyes, soft chocolate-brown
fur...
And it's all coming from that box!

Alysia McNeil (12)
Co-Operative Academy Failsworth, Failsworth

Shockingly Evil And Vile

From the perspective of Ted Bundy

I sat in the cell,
A bright orange blinding my eyes
And still in my ears
I could hear the piercing cries.
More than one, more than five,
It could've been her or you.
It could have been a pregnant woman,
With a child no older than two.
Before I did what I did,
I was no more than an average Joe,
Now no one in America can say
My name they do not know.
I want them to call me a martyr,
Or maybe even a saint
And when I have been executed,
In my blood they will paint
My name over and over,
Some may call me a disgrace.
"Extremely wicked, shockingly evil and vile."
Their words have no place.
'Ted Bundy! Ted Bundy!'
The news headlines will cry
And everyone reads, willingly disgusted
And this is my last goodbye.
For my message is my body

And my soul is my crime
And the prison guard is here,
It appears I'm out of time.
So let me go, let me die,
Let your hearts fill with joy,
Though I am 'heinous' and 'inhumane'
Deep down I am just a boy.
I am not sorrowful, but reminiscent.
What more would you expect?
I have deceived and murdered and so much more
But in my heart, there is no regret.

Arren Mitchell-Kew (14)
Co-Operative Academy Failsworth, Failsworth

Untitled

"She!"
The voices chant in his head,
The teases that just won't stop,
The tears that stained his bed,
Constantly questioning life.

"She!"
Fabric binding his chest,
Teens mocking his every move.
"It's just a phase," she tried to convince him.
She would never understand the tears shed.

"She!"
His heart thumped in his chest,
The sound of a razor penetrated his ears.

Beep, beep, beep!
The alarm rang, forcing him awake.
Just a dream? No.
"Born a girl, always a girl."

Lucie Waterhouse (12)
Co-Operative Academy Failsworth, Failsworth

Boom!

My vision crept slowly back to me,
People around me were screaming in agony
But I couldn't hear.
Only fleeting glimpses of chaos.
Pain.
I felt like my soul had been ripped from my body,
Only to be forcefully shoved back
As I tried desperately to cry for help.
Something was there...
What was it?
My hands were shaking uncontrollably,
My ears were ringing,
My body was in anguish.
All I could hear was:
"Take cover! Take cover! There is a-"
Boom!

Oliver Barber (13)
Ipswich School, Ipswich

Life Of A Computer

Every weekday, when my power button is pressed,
Sighs of tiredness and yawns of boredom are the first things
my half-conscious machinery hears
Followed by rapid typing and clicking
Of speeds only achieved by a well-trained typist
Or a stressed businessman
Chasing the deadline for his still-unfinished document.

Sighs and yawns from minutes before
Are replaced with laughter at an occasional funny meme.
Constant calls of, "Come eat dinner!" from a frustrated
mother
Are answered with a calm, almost cold, "Later."
Knocks on a desperate door,
Which fears for its safety after becoming a punchbag,
Are met with the apparent, "Doing homework," lies
That only a certain president calling climate change 'a hoax'
Could even attempt to execute and expect success.

Is that what teenage life is like?

Long sessions of YouTube bingeing
Replaced with ignorant random memes
And the kind of dark humour
That only twisted individuals extract enjoyment from.
Afternoons in playgrounds replaced
With long hours of endless clicking and tapping from the
isolation of online games.

Every weekday
The sighs of tiredness and yawns of boredom...

Perhaps it *is* what teenage life is like.

Marcus Luk (14)
Ipswich School, Ipswich

The Moors

The thick brown of the carpet laid before me
Filled my vision.
Its twisting, uneven mass squeezed and choked at the rocks
and ravines.
As I hung there, suspended above the writhing limbs of
desiccated ferns,
I felt the breeze.
A breeze that had descended many a valley
And had filled, with its cooling comfort, many a forest.
But it was here that it was at its strongest,
Trying to force every feather, every straining muscle
Off of my delicate frame.
I shifted my form,
Bracing for the invisible form that was yet to envelop me.
Its powerful arms pushed at me,
Encouraging my rigid wings to relax and let them fall.
I didn't fall.
I had repeated this scenario thousands of times,
Its soothing touch and its persuasive push did not fool me.
I shouted at it.
Mocking the thought that it could ever doom me.
A raven!
This little tickle thought, it could condemn a raven!
But I knew this moment of blissful victory was all too short.
It knew it too.
With a roar, it focused its whole strength at me,

Sending me clumsily flapping at its lifeless brother
Down, down to the ferns below.
They slowly bent, gently cradling my defeated form.
They stared at me, puzzled.
I could almost feel their disappointment...

Oliver Williams (13)
Ipswich School, Ipswich

Daily Routine Of A Tree

This is where I live,
Thousands of people walk past me every day,
Animals climb up me
And some live in me.
But that's just who I am,
A plain old tree.

I've been here for centuries,
In the same exact place every day.
I have seen everything,
From people crying
To people falling in love.
This is my purpose.

This is what I am here for,
A shoulder to cry on,
A friend to lean on,
Here to comfort people in times of need.
It's just me,
An ordinary tree.

I look over people,
Watch how they grow,
Right in front of my eyes.
Most of them turn into amazing people
And as I get older, they get wiser.

But they have to learn not to destroy me,
Soon I will not be here.
No shoulder to cry on,
No friend to lean on.
My home and my existence -
Gone.

Charley Butler (13)
Ipswich School, Ipswich

Prey At Night

The wind rushes my fur as I creep up to the buffalo.
My ligaments elegantly brushing against my bristled fur.
My burnt flame terracotta mane blowing in my face.
The prowling pace I am going at is disguising me in the dry grass.
Keeping low, no one must know I'm here.
Seeing my prey in the distance makes my mouth water.
They aren't alert!
As my paws beat the ground,
The scent gets stronger with every bound.
The savannah vast with the herd of buffalo
Where my eyes are fixated.
Daringly, I head for the horns.
Quickening, I hastily aggravate the buffalo.
Now attached to the broad back,
I battle the beast.
Grabbing the hide.
My claws make him buck.
I have defeated the animal.
No one to save him now.
He lays on the grassland, gasping for his last breath.
Waiting for the hyena to close in...

Evie Montgomery (11)
Ipswich School, Ipswich

End This Nightmare

Is it hot in here, or is it just me?
Am I the only one who can't breathe?
Where on earth did my family go?
I just can't remember when I last saw snow.
It's been a while since I felt a cool breeze
Trickling through my dried-up leaves.
All these scared creatures cry out, hastily,
"Humans are coming!" I offer them safety.
Until the day I hear the saws
I know that I will feel no more.
I'm not afraid (well, not for me),
I am afraid of what will be.
My life means nought, I'll give it up
But when will the humans think, *enough!*
We have done way too much damage!
And will they find a way to manage?
Do what you will to me, I really don't care
But humans, please change your ways,
End this nightmare.

Olivia Walker (14)
Ipswich School, Ipswich

The King Of The Jungle?

To live in the jungle is a game,
A game of life or death,
The only way to win
Is to have power.

I am the king,
The king of this game;
The king of power,
I am the king of the jungle.

Living in the jungle is a game,
But this game is coming to an end,
My jungle is coming to an end,
I will come to an end.

I have faced many competitors
And I am still the king,
But I have a new competitor
Who is willing to destroy my jungle.

All animals obey me,
All but my competitor,
This animal doesn't care about my jungle -
Only itself.

Destruction has spread through my jungle,
Spreading like the plague,
Burning to a crisp,

All because of this one animal...
Humans.

Bethany Quinn (13)
Ipswich School, Ipswich

Animal Kingdom: Poaching

Silence is blazing at the crack of dawn,
The moon's crescent still blooming in the paint of blue.
The world is awake.
Whilst arching down as slow as a sloth
To have some cold water,
Like warm soothing milk in the morning,
I look upon his horn reaching over my forehead,
Feeling proud.

Suddenly, a golden digit spins past my head,
Raging my back legs, I stampede over to
The silhouette of a man in the distance.
Dancing around like I'm in a disco,
I run around, dodging the bullets flying at me
From all angles!

Something strikes me just below my chest,
The black figure close up goes by the name Herbie.
A man with an evil snarl,
Next thing I know,
I'm looking down from the clouds at this evil planet.

Herbie Shaw (11), Reuben Alty & Archie Kinsman
Ipswich School, Ipswich

We Need To Regain Our Pride

Humans often talk about pride,
Apparently they have lots of it.
These people are delusional.
We have lost our rights
Over the years.
We have lost it in the most disgraceful manner.
They talk about being the saviours
When they are the destroyers.

They have destroyed our pride
Through their treatment of living things
Which have the same rights of enjoying
This world as we do.

How could they have disgraced us in this manner?
We,
Not just our country,
But our world,
Need to fight for this pride.
Drive these disgusting people to suffering.
Give them a life they deserve.
Prison.
Death.
We need sacrifice,
We need justice,
We need to restore our pride.

Solomon Belshaw (13)
Ipswich School, Ipswich

Locked

I am a visitor in my own mind;
Trapped, caged, confined.
Darkness eats me
Until I break,
Until I can't hold it in,
Until it's finally over.

Don't leave without seeing all the colours,
Look into my heart, feel my burn.
Bruised, aching, sore,
A face in a crowd,
Drowning in my own mind.

The truth is twisted,
Taken away on a journey.
Our destination is a lie,
One that spins out of control,
Into a world we cannot escape.

Through their eyes, I am untroubled.
Through their eyes, I am unsuccessful.
Through their eyes, I am carefree, fulfilled, complete.

Through their eyes, I am different.

Rowan Calver (14)
Ipswich School, Ipswich

Ambition

I woke up one morning to find myself still tired,
I yawned so wide I could have swallowed a tyre!
I slowly slithered from the warmth of my bed,
Onto the carpet, I laid my head.
From this position, the world seemed clearer,
In years to come, I would become a road sweep cleaner!

My thoughts turned to the day ahead,
My body was filled with dread!
As my eyes flitted around my bed,
I suddenly realised what my teacher said:
"You, young man, should know better,
Your homework's shabby,
You could do better.
If you spent less time dreaming
And looking at the ceiling,
You could turn your hand to office cleaning!"

Hector Bishop-Penn (13)
Ipswich School, Ipswich

Motionless

The malicious object strangled my throat;
I gasped for air.
The cold fire inside me
Burned, consuming all happiness
As my heart laid motionless on the sand;
Waves crashed.

Vanishing, the air was suffocating.
Melancholy cloaked me.
Exasperation drenched me.
My breathing became more frantic
As my soul laid motionless on the sand.
Wind whispered.

Beautiful pebbles were replaced with monsters,
Killing my family.
They would:
Trap,
Suffocate,
Until they were satisfied.

And now it was happening to me.

My body laid motionless on the sand;
Hearts broken.

Beatrice Noordhuis (11) & Evelyn
Ipswich School, Ipswich

A Leaf Is What I Am

I am a leaf, hanging from a branch,
I am a leaf, caught in the wind,
I am a leaf, floating and falling,
I am a leaf, and a leaf is what I am.

I am a leaf, laying on the ground,
I am a leaf, waiting to be stood on,
I am a leaf, imagining the end,
I am a leaf, and a leaf is what I am.

I am a leaf, all alone,
I am a leaf, with no home,
I am a leaf, sad and lonely,
I am a leaf, and a leaf is what I am.

I am a leaf, curling and dying,
I am a leaf, wanting a friend,
I am a leaf, first green, now brown,
I am a leaf, and a leaf is what I am.

Leonidas Holburn (11)

Ipswich School, Ipswich

Endangered

I wake up in the morning breeze,
The wind whistling through the autumn leaves.

The sound of a lion's roar
Echoing through the morning dawn.

The grass blowing through the plain
That sounds like evening rain.

As I trudge through the mud
It starts to become a wasteful flood.

All is quiet except for a click
I don't have time to think
As I find my feet, all is still
A gunshot becomes a kill.
I fall back in the flood
I find myself in watery mud.

What could they possibly want from me?
Because of all this, I am no more...

Rafe Chapman (11) & Henry Rutland
Ipswich School, Ipswich

Send Help!

From light to dark,
From colour to bland,
From life to death.

When once I lived to support all life,
Now all life's gone; I have lost my will.
These new things came with two long tails and lights,
Their flashing tools and dark desires took all
My joy away. They left me stranded here,
Yet under the waves I dwell;
Slowly I wither until there's nothing but hell.
Once the damage was done, they never returned,
I was left, a turtle lacking a shell.
My hub of life destroyed,
Where these awful entities came from.
I am afraid it's too late for me...

Oliver Kinsman (14)
Ipswich School, Ipswich

Life

Out of one of my eyes, I finally see hope,
I have been on the streets for so long
A human comes to see me,
I think I have found a home.

It is too good for reality,
Finally, I will be fed,
Instead of longing for scraps,
I think I have found a home.

My shrivelled eyes won't hold me back,
My four stick-like legs have never been stronger,
The saviour of my life leads me to my destiny,
I think I have found a home.

I am old but in paradise,
Life wasn't so bad after all,
I wither away happily,
I have found a home.

George Collis (11) & Samuel
Ipswich School, Ipswich

The View Of A President

My beloved fans, cheering for what is right,
Raising signs of love, asking for change.
Red caps lay on their heads,
A symbol of their belief in me.

On the opposite side, it's a different world
Full of hate and signs of anger.
They scream at me, say I'm an idiot,
I don't understand, what have I done?

A wall divides them, shutting them off,
Preventing them from ending this war.
Will this ever stop, will they ever agree?
Or will I be hated forever?

Barbara Skorczak (11), Lily & Francesca
Ipswich School, Ipswich

Prisoner

From the perspective of Nelson Mandela

I may only have an iron bed, but
My soul softens the sheets.
Ribbons of music dance through my head

Whispering with my every move.
It screeches and clangs
Until it turns into a comforting
Melody.

I cry out in determination
And break through my
Restraining bars,
I run across the soft, sandy African plains.

Yet I am still in my bed,
With the small slit of a
Window.

Held back only by the metal jail bars.

Amaya Du Preez (11)
Ipswich School, Ipswich

Have You Ever Heard The Roar Of A Lion?

Have you ever heard a roar of a lion?
Powerful.
Powerful like the gaze of a glorified king,
Majestic.
Majestic like the voices of a unified choir,
Proud.
Proud like the tallest tree, hovering over the open plains.
I have heard the roar of a lion,
I heard it once and it repeats in my head over and over.
My fondest memory.

Victor Tocca (15)
Ipswich School, Ipswich

We Will Remember Them

Her name was Alisha
And I am alone.

World War One was a place of death,
The marching as loud as thunder,
Barbed wire as sharp as knives,
Falling dominoes that replaced the buildings,
Puddles of blood formed soldiers in their stead,
Whistling bombs shaped the sky.

The soldiers were scared to death,
The swirling battlefield in the sky,
When dark clouds smouldered into red,
We will remember them.
When the dying soldiers shift their heads,
We will remember them.

Two minutes' silence for the dead,
She thought of the fields when they were red,
Red not with poppies
But with blood,
The blood of men,
The image of death.

Two minutes' silence for the dead,
She stood in the crowd and bowed her head,
Not in reverence but in shame
At the insult, in memory of their name.

Two minutes' silence for the dead,
The last post is sounding
And eyes are red,
But Reveille is sounding for her instead
Of the post in memory of the dead.
Together, we will remember them.

Her name was Alisha
And I was alone,
But she helped me remember that I was a soldier

And that I was never alone.

Alisha Lea (14)
Prenton High School For Girls, Rock Ferry

Why Was I There?

I dozed into a dream of something so unreal,
I was flying high in the sky in a Hawker Typhoon,
Soaring above the lands of World War II.
Why was I there?

I was alone in the peaceful sky,
Flying higher than the clouds
In an everlasting blue lagoon.
Why was I there?

I heard guns blazing
And bombs of doom,
I was hit and was going down too.
Why was I there?

I spiralled in my Hawker,
Hurtling towards the derelict landscape,
Like a fiery shooting star.
Why was I there?

I braced for impact,
Whilst attempting to gain control,
But all attempts were failing.
Why was I there?

I exploded into a fiery flame
And the Hawker smashed into the ground,
With my body disintegrating on impact.
Why was I there?

I saw darkness and death,
But a light came towards me
And I knew it was time.
Why was I there?

I suddenly awoke,
Dazed and confused,
Wondering what I had just experienced.
Why was I there?

Why was I there?
Why me?
Why was I... there?
Why me?

Alex Hampson (14)
Prenton High School For Girls, Rock Ferry

To Society

To society,
We were just jewellery,
Something to flaunt.
A bargaining chip in business,
A mother,
An object.

To society,
How would it feel if we unearthed our voices?
If we became something more -
More independent,
More valiant,
More than just a woman.

To society,
'Deeds, not words'.
A motto we live by.
Something to stand for.
Something to live for.
Something to die for.

To society,
'Votes for women'.
A thing we wanted.
A thing we should have the right to.
A thing we need to make us equal.

To society,
If one of us died,
Would you cry?
Would you be shocked?

Would you finally notice us?

Ellie Oates (14)
Prenton High School For Girls, Rock Ferry

Mother Earth

I give you what you need:
Trees, water, food.
You wouldn't want to leave.

I give you the largest of rainforests,
To the smallest of ponds.
I give you seas undiscovered.
I give you peaks above the clouds.

All you do is take.
I'm an actor on the world's stage,
I'm being transformed
Into a plastic junkyard,
Waiting for my final curtain call.

Destroy the humans I say,
Destroy them,
They're killing me off anyway.

But there's a way to fix me.
There is still a way.
You just need to take care of me,
Stop overheating me.
You need to act fast before I

Fade away.

Lucy Call (14)
Prenton High School For Girls, Rock Ferry

The Pills Are It

Addiction is everything,
Life depends on it.
At the cost of anything,
Pills are it.

No matter where I get them,
Any reason for it,
Anything for the feel of them,
Pills are it.

Never mind the cost
For the chance to enhance it.
Who cares about the loss?
Pills are it.

Blend with the crowd, they say,
Feel like I'm not myself without it.
Some days I just pray -
I don't want the pill to be it.

Too far now,
Hurt too many with it.
I need the help now,
I wish the pills aren't it.

White flag,
End of this journey.
Getting help now,
Pills aren't it.

Chloe Stormont (14)
Prenton High School For Girls, Rock Ferry

Elephants Never Forget

We never forget what you've done to us.
Torn out our trunks until we bled;
Bled into the sand, the grass, our waterholes,
Left for dead in our own land.

And yet we can only plead.
We can silently plead,
Our eyes filling with dread
As you approach us with your machinery.

We can remember, we always remember
Our friends used as trophies;
Trophies of death, viewed by you as only
A mere accomplishment.

Are you happy now?
Happy about the pain that you've caused?
The suffering thrown upon us?
We have so many burdens now.

We never forget what you've done to us.

Kai Maclean (14)
Prenton High School For Girls, Rock Ferry

I feel the bacteria creeping onto me.
I need to be clean.
I need to wash myself again.
I can't help it.

I can't help it.
You offer me food
And I inspect the dirty plate.
I suspect you're confused, but
I can't help it.

I can't help it.
My family tell me to go outside.
I can't do that.
Do they not understand what's out there?
I can't help it.

I can't help it.
Everything needs to be clean.
Stainless and spotless.
That's how I love everything to be.
I can't help it.

Angel Elizabeth Brothers (14)
Prenton High School For Girls, Rock Ferry

Thirty Women

From the perspective of Ted Bundy

She was gorgeous,
She gave me that look
That almost made me nauseous.
She was just sitting there reading a book.
Thirty women.

She was pretty,
I could feel her presence.
She was witty,
The look she gave me was pleasant.
Thirty women.

She was lovely,
She was caring,
She seemed comfy,
All the boys were staring.
Thirty women.

Times it by ten,
They were never undressed alive.
You won't get the outcome from *when*
But *how* many women died.
Thirty women.

Alex Roberts (13)
Prenton High School For Girls, Rock Ferry

Will They?

Scared, nervous, worried.
Will they kick me again?
Will they punch me again?
Will they call me names again?
Will they?

Scared, nervous, worried.
Suddenly, it stopped.
Why is the world white?
The pain instantly stopped.

Scared, nervous, worried.
I want to go home
With my family
But all I see is white and nothing else...

Sheila Negmadin (13)
Prenton High School For Girls, Rock Ferry

The Mind Of A Teenage Girl

We are teenage girls
We try to hide the hurt and pain
But know that suicide will call again
The things they say, they cut so deep
And make you want to take that leap
The leap that then will end it all
But is it really worth the fall?

We are teenage girls
The late-night tears and arguments
And midnight calls to the one you love
You feel so numb and don't know how
You've managed to cope up to now

We are teenage girls
We accept the roses and ignore the thorns
We just want him to stay
We bottle up the pain
And pray it goes away
Our heads, they spin and swirl and scatter
We are just teenage girls and we truly do not matter

We are teenage girls
When we go home, the pinned curls are put up in a messy bun
And we stare back at our reflection and wonder what we have become
Our fake smile has faded

The tears continue to fall
And once again, feel nothing at all

We are teenage girls
We have no tears left to cry
We've been broken down and used
Each day is like a chore
And every minute, every hour breaks you more and more

We are teenage girls
What is beautiful?
How do you accept a compliment you don't believe?
How can you be beautiful if you can't tick every box?
To have a skinny waist and long, thick hair
And be defined by what you wear
From dinner dates to being seen as shark bait
Don't conceal, just let him in?
And feel him up against your skin?
You bear the pain
You learn to cope
And on their hurtful words, you choke

We are teenage girls
And you don't know our story
The lies
The pain
The fall
The hurt
Don't let them in

Don't let them see
The girl you truly want to be

We are teenage girls.

Nieve Barr (13)
Stokesley School, Stokesley

Mirror, Mirror

Mirror, mirror on the wall,
Why do you show us fat and small?
Hair not quite right and imperfect skin?
No wonder we feel we don't fit in.

One lump here, one bump there,
Every day just anguish and despair,
When will that reflection we see
Be as perfect as those on TV?

Inch by inch, we pick apart
Those parts of us that break our hearts.
The pressure and expectation of who we should be
Burns a hole in any joy or glee.

How did this all-consuming self-war start?
The constant worthlessness and tearing apart?
We keep it quiet so as not to annoy.
But this comparison game is a thief of joy.

Mirror, mirror on the wall,
What is perfection after all?

Molly Butterfield
Stokesley School, Stokesley

Tragic Phenomenons Across The Earth

The face of the Earth shakes
Thundering across land and seas for miles on end
People run in fear, shock, confusion
But...
They have no idea what's to come
Then...

Screams start becoming apparent from the far distance
Getting louder and louder and louder!
Crash... bang!
Buildings. Trees. Rocks. The lot
All start collapsing and there is no escape but...
The slippery slope to a tragic death.

When things couldn't get any worse
Splash!
A colossal tsunami the size of Burj Khalia and more
Just hit the shore and isn't stopping
It swallows people up like it's no big deal
No one, *no one* can stop it or do anything
You may as well give up, it's a death sentence!

But when things can't get any worse
Boom!
A volcano erupts
A flume of lava that's smoking hot is pushing and bullying you
Closer to disaster

There is no turning back, you can only go with it.

You take a look at Antarctica, now it's there
In ten years it's gone, flooding everywhere
It can happen to polar bears, penguins
Dying one after another
Left, right and centre.
Global problems increasing daily
Your life not liveable
Only survival till your fate is decided.

The only thing you can do is sit and watch
But wonder why we ignored it and didn't make a change
Now you are paying the price.
There won't be animal extinction but human extinction
And no one can stop it or do anything.

William Firman (13)
Stokesley School, Stokesley

Masked

A deadly disease,
It takes over our lives,
The media, it changes us,
It fakes us.
This wall I hide behind is getting too tall.

This isn't me,
This can't be me,
I'll never see myself the same again.
This mask is becoming too much of a task.

Thousands of followers,
This isn't what I want,
The pressure hits me like a speeding train.
But still, this wall I hide behind is getting too tall.

What can I do?
Where can I go?
There's nowhere to run.

In 2017 alone, 5,821 suicides were recorded,
One third of them were
Because of this monster we call
Social media.

Emily Rhodes (13)
Stokesley School, Stokesley

Lost In Music

Music takes me away
To a place of the unknown,
The magic melody
Chills through my bone.

Psychedelic rock
Makes the Earth spin,
When I'm lost in the music
My soul is within.

Waiting for the band to perform
My heart skips a beat,
As the night becomes day
I am still dancing on my feet.

Putting on my headphones
The rap blasting in my ears,
Just listening to the lyrics
Nearly brings me to tears.

Music is all around us
There is never any silence,
So many different sounds
Music is timeless.

Polly Hunter (13)
Stokesley School, Stokesley

Let Out The Lie, Trap In The Truth

You may feel safe now but you know
They will come for you
And they will always prevail.
The dreaded pound upon the door
That will come when you
Are least expecting it and
At last, I can rest.

Twelve years spent sitting in silence
Staring into nothingness, serenaded by
The soft sighs of scared souls.
Watching the rain drip bit by bit
Down the windowpane, running away
Just like you when
At last, I can rest.

Like on a long-forgotten sports day
The sun glared at everyone
The school no longer a sea of blue
But a multicoloured fiesta of people.
I was running, running, running
The crowds flew by and then, suddenly
At last, I could rest.

Within these four walls, I am alone
Accompanied only by the
Murmurs of murky memories
Resurfacing after hours of patient toil

This will happen to you too
When the knocking comes and
At last, I can rest.

Listen to my warning, drifting slowly
Towards you and then you'll know
I am innocent; that it's you who
Should be sitting here, not me
They didn't listen to the truth then
But they will now have the body so
At last, I can rest.

Hana Jones (13)
Stokesley School, Stokesley

Truth Be Told

Truth be told,
On paper of gold.

A priceless piece,
Of wonders that cease.

You cannot buy,
What's worse than a lie.

As a matter of fact,
It's better to act

Than find out the truth hidden beneath,
It's worse than pulling a sword from a sheath.

Especially when you're on the other end,
That's when you may need a helping friend.

Sometimes it spins out of control
And then you meet a bitter, bad troll.

That troll, of course, is that lie
That's gone and blinded you in the eye.

Amy Lewis (12)
Stokesley School, Stokesley

Waiting

I hear a train,
Everyone gets excited,
Could cause them pain,
But still they try to be delighted.

As the train pulls up, soldiers are waving,
Reality starts to take place,
Some smiles are fading,
I can see it blow up in someone's face.

Wives begin to cry,
Sons start to shake,
They never got to say goodbye,
Feel as if they might break.

Wounds are devastating,
Feel like they are suffocating,
Now hearts are elevating,
I will never stop waiting.

Gabriella Mathers (13)
Stokesley School, Stokesley

Darkness

I can feel it when the lights turn off
The presence that builds up around me
I can feel it twisting and turning around me as I quiver in the corner
The darkness pulls me in and I feel like I can't stop it

I am not afraid of the dark

I try to explain to people what it is like
But nobody will understand
I know that things are the same when the sun goes down
And I know that I am safe when I am in my bed

I can feel it when the lights turn off
The tension that builds up around me
I can feel someone brush my shoulder
The shadows leaning over me

I am not afraid of anything

I try to ignore the whispers in the dark
But I know they are there
I know that they are calling me to the darkness
And I know I don't want to go there

I can feel it when the lights turn off
The breath on the left side of my neck
I can feel them tapping on my bedroom walls
The never-ending nightmare

I am not afraid of the dark
I am afraid of what is *in* the dark.

Grace Eve Roberts (13)
Stokesley School, Stokesley

I Try

I try but I'll never be perfect
I smile but it's not really worth it
Deep down, I know I don't deserve it
I try but I'll never be perfect

I hide all my tears on the inside
No one can ever know what I hide
I can't tell you how many times I've lied
I hide all my tears on the inside

I wish I could pull me apart
Erase the ugly and only leave the heart
I wish I could cut me in half
I wish I could pull me apart

I've tried my hardest to fix how I look
I've tried every trick in the book
The healthy meals I've tried to cook
I've tried my hardest to fix how I look

I try but I'll never love myself
The perfect me is someone else
I'm trying but I might need some help
I try but I'll never love myself

I cry but nobody's there to notice
I just want someone to know this
But deep down, I can't help but show this
I cry but nobody's there to notice.

Leon Moody (13)
Stokesley School, Stokesley

But You Stand And Stare

Fire devouring everything in its path,
Trees decaying,
But you stand and stare.

You leave a trail of plastic everywhere you go
And every year 100,000 marine creatures die because of
plastic.
But you don't do anything.

You kill rhinos just for their horns,
Why do you do this? Is it just for vengeance?
But you stand and stare.

Animals full of sorrow,
Animals fading away.
But you don't do anything.

Animals defeated,
Humans victorious.
But you stand and stare.

Open your eyes,
Look around you.
Animals are becoming extinct because of us.
But you don't do anything.

Bethany Hill (13)
Stokesley School, Stokesley

The Fight

I couldn't believe my eyes
The things that I could see
All the fighting near me
It gave me so much fear

They punched and they kicked
As if it was a war
The bully and the bullied
They fight until they fall

He called him weird and sniggered
And said, "You have so much fear,
You look like you are going to cry."
"But I don't want to shed a tear."

He said, "You're so small,
So small you can't punch till I fall.
You're the one that's going to fall,
Fall against the wall..."

Jack Doyle (13)
Stokesley School, Stokesley

The Comment

I was sat there
Trembling under the covers
Thinking about what she said at school
Checking my phone, the worst was yet to come
And there it was, for everyone to see
The one bullet which would kill
Was now public
There was a comment
The pain worsened and became sharper
'What a fat s***'
I sat there bawling out
Hurt... hurt severely
With no bandage to close the wound
It stayed with me like a scar.

Harley Norton-Moore (14)
Stokesley School, Stokesley

Help!

Manchester was bouncing
Like a trampoline,
Listening to the music,
I was very keen.
Then it all went downhill,
I could hear the word 'kill'.
Boom! Boom! Boom!
Someone flew right past me
And slammed into a wall,
It felt like the floor opened up and caused a great fall.
Soon there was rubble everywhere,
People screaming, crying.
139 wounded,
23 dead
And I woke up in a hospital bed.

Alex Bone (13)
Stokesley School, Stokesley

Lost

In some ways I'm glad
In others I'm sad
The iceberg melted
I'm sure I felt it

They all got lost
Like a piece of post
My family gone
Lost like my home

It's the humans' fault
My ears are full of salt
Carbon released
Like a terrible beast

Please help me
I don't want to lose all that's dear to me
I don't want to die
To horrible humans
Letting carbon loose.

Edward Lambert (13)
Stokesley School, Stokesley

Men Are In Charge

You're standing, looking out the window,
Locked up, doing chores,
Never time
To hear about the changes
Going on in the world.
The men are in charge.

My mama always said,
"Stay home,
Do the chores,
The men are in charge."

I wanted an education,
Papa said no,
"Woman are for housework,
The men are in charge."

Well, look at me now,
Standing proud,
Standing strong,
I've got a job, I've got a home
And I haven't
Got a husband.
But still,
The men are in charge.

I'm afraid it's a dream,
I pinch myself and see

It is.
The men are in charge.

My papa is looking at me,
I know what he is thinking
And I don't care.
The men are in charge.

Last night, my brother came home from school,
He bragged about his education
And moaned about it too,
Then he started to boss me about.
The men are in charge.

I'm fed up,
Last night I watched TV,
Donald Trump again,
The sexist president from the USA
And to him,
The men are in charge.

Last night, my friend came over,
His name is Jack,
He told me education's boring,
He told me I was lucky,
So I called him sexist,
He told me my life is great,
He told me,
"Men are in charge."

Well, look at me now,
Standing proud,
Standing strong,
I've got a job,
I've got a home

And I haven't got a husband.

The men aren't in charge.

Libby Attwood (11)
Tamworth Enterprise College, Belgrave

Mental Health

Just imagine being that one child,
That one child who thinks differently to others.
Just imagine being that one child who controls themselves
and reacts differently to everyone else.
Things like bullying only happen because they're different to
others.
Everybody's different
But they shouldn't have to walk the streets
Or corridors at school
And get treated differently.
This affects people a lot, bullying
And just having this one issue,
It affects your whole life.

Okay, put yourself in the parents' shoes,
This doesn't just affect the child but also the parents.
Being that parent when your child comes home and has had
a miserable day,
Because they are either being bullied
People are making fun of them,
Just because they think or do things different
To all the other children.
"It's not fair!" they say to you
Then your heart thumps out of your chest,
Feeling all emotional because your child is being treated
differently.
Because they do things different.

Charlie Winyard (11)
Tamworth Enterprise College, Belgrave

Equality/Bullying

Walking down the corridor
Another nine insults hit her.
"Carrot head!"
"Eat some more."
"How many carrots do you eat?"
"You look so depressed."
"Ginger!"
Every word hitting her harder than the last.

She looked like she was on the edge.
Every day more painful than the last.
She hated herself
For how unnaturally skinny she was,
She was teased for her hair colour.
She wanted to dye it more than anything.
My parents say it is lucky, cool and beautiful for being ginger,
They never said it came with this pain for her.

Thoughts rushed through her mind,
Panic filled her body
Year Seven to Year Eleven.
What's the point anymore?
Everybody hates me.
Why don't I just end it all?
I'm a waste of time,
I'm a waste of space.

Walking down the corridor,
But this time no insults.
Nine questions were asked with peace.
"Why did you try to end it?"
She just cried, nothing was holding her back.
There was no point hiding it,
The beloved nurse rushed out in tears,
The nurse was shocked.
She could not believe her ears,
How much this little girl had gone through,
That she tried ending it all.

Rose Giles (14)

Tamworth Enterprise College, Belgrave

The Rapper Dave's Identity

Writing a song about being black for the industry
Brought out my true personality.
Feeling like a bullet getting aimed at by racists
From preschool to nursery
To primary then secondary
Dealing with the same issues from day to day
Time to make awareness my way.

Growing up in this world without a voice
Makes my heart beast faster than a run.
Hearing the same haters hating on the skin colour black
In my opinion, black is beautiful
And there's not a thing I would change about it.
That's why I wrote this song
With my experience of it stated in facts.

Teaching the young right from wrong
After a long period of time has already gone.
Being black is something special
If you make it worth the while.
My dark skin colour stands out against the light blue sky
Shining bright.

Love who you are and be proud
Even if you don't have a large crowd.
Be inspired but be careful on the streets
As anything can happen to you and me.

We're different, which is good
Don't doubt, even if you feel unloved.
People will always hate and be horrible
But us black people can change that
As we still have a long while.

Keira Vallery O'Connell (13)
Tamworth Enterprise College, Belgrave

A Life Beyond The Human Race

Medium,
But
Feeling small,
Black as soil
But
White as a cloud,
I am fun to play with.

I am a dog
Called Bo,
I am a miniature breed
With beautiful brown eyes.

Crash!
Oops!
I broke a plate in this kitchen.
Can I get away with it with my cuteness?

I need my owners
To give me attention and food.
Will she snitch on me?

I am a dog
With not the best behaviour.

But I am a dog.
What do you expect?
I am getting older
As the days go by.

Even though we playfight
We act like loving siblings,
She is amazing.

I have never been the best,
But this is what I am.
She plays with me,
She cuddles me,
She wants me.

I feel small by how quick she grows,
I eat quick like a cheetah, though.

Medium,
But
Feeling small,
Black as soil,
White as a cloud,
I am fun to play with.

The more I growl,
I feel loved.

I am adorable,
But not the best-behaved.

I hope you enjoy my life,
Even though I have strife.

Erin Royston (11)
Tamworth Enterprise College, Belgrave

Yoshi

What are we doing y'all?
Killing harmless creatures,
Dumping them all over the place,
Never being able to do what they want.

The creature never eats what it likes,
Always eating stuff to help the player.
At least they get to be healthy.
But they have to eat killers.

Why do we bully them?
Don't chuck them down holes.
What have they done?
They shouldn't deserve it.

Mario always hitting them on the head,
That's not pleasant.
The creature probably has a bruise,
He shouldn't get hit just to stick his tongue out.

He's a dinosaur,
He's a dinosaur,
A friend to Mario?
How is that possible?

Why is he tortured?
He has done nothing.
Mario is the one,
Torture him instead.

Who is controlling him?
The players, of course.

Let him do his own stuff,
Not Mario's work.

When Mario was a baby,
Who was there?
Yoshi, not his parents.
Yoshi shouldn't be the parent.

Mario called him Yoshi,
But I call him Green Broccoli!

Bobby Hickey (11)
Tamworth Enterprise College, Belgrave

Countdown

I'm already a dead man
Waiting for my time to come,
I feel like a circus animal
Isolated in a metal cage.
What am I doing here?
Eating dinner with strangers,
Paedophiles and rapists,
When I should be home with my family.

I'm already a dead man,
Why should I have to put up with this trash every day?
I'm waiting for my time to come.
Do I deserve this? To be in here,
A hellhole of a place...
But I'm only human,
I can make a mistake,
I can make a mistake because it's normal,
But I'm not normal.
That's why I'm here.

I'm already a dead man,
I was found guilty...
Now I'm going insane.
The detectives messed up my evidence
And announced the false information.
Why me?
Why should I be in this situation?

What have I done?

I'm already a dead man
In my cell, waiting to be found,
Just a matter of time,
It's like a countdown.

Ethan Winfield (13)
Tamworth Enterprise College, Belgrave

Imagine This

Imagine this...
You're on square one,
You go to school to learn,
Not to cry, misbehave, gossip or laugh about the sad girl.
You only know half of it!

Imagine this...
You're the sad girl,
You're there to learn,
Not to get put down by the people who discriminate you.
There's a fire inside your heart,
But it can't show because you're scared that they will put it out
With a sea of fear and confusion.

Imagine this...
Your fear is spreading,
Spreading faster than a disease,
It can't get any worse,
You painfully tell yourself.
How how can it not?
You're eating lunch on a toilet, for God's sake!

Imagine this...
Everyone hates you,
Or so you think,
Walking through the hallway is like laying on a bed of nails.
Pain!

Imagine this...
You're back to square one,
You go to school to learn
And that's what you do...

Kiera Elisabeth Bate (12)

Tamworth Enterprise College, Belgrave

The Deadly Twist Of Momo Yaoyorozu

The snow-haired female walked into her home,
Covered in bruises, scars and other wounds
She saw her father on the chair
Asleep and surrounded by beer bottles,
She forced a smile as she saw,
The female then rushed upstairs, leaving her smile behind.

She stared...

She stared into the sky-cloud mirror
Her eyes a bloodshed red
She began again
It began again.

The voices screamed and wailed
The female flooded like a fountain.

She smashed the glass, screaming,
"Leave me alone!"
Her hands turned red as well as her face
Causing calmness once again,
She smiled as she wrote:

'It's hard being me,
It's hard being like this,
My white hands now stained with blood,
Soon too will be yours.'

Droplets of water fell,
Her eyes now a mixture of purple and red,
Her white stained by the monster,
The monster she created.

Jaimeelei Bridgwater (12)
Tamworth Enterprise College, Belgrave

Our Home

Everybody keeps saying this is 'our' Earth
Well, that's where you've got it wrong!
We are so quick to say someone else is wrong,
Yet we struggle to say
When it is actually us who made the mistake.
So many times I've been told
To clean up my mess,
Well, now that we young ones have not made any mess,
They're leaving us to clean up theirs.

So many things we've made from animals:
Pianos, medicines and many things that means they die.
And now the Earth is dying,
We are trying to separate.
Donald Trump's trying to build a wall,
The UK's trying to leave Europe,
That's not what we need.
We need to come together
To save the Earth.
If anything impossible is gonna happen,
It's gonna happen here.

We say enslaving someone is a monstrosity,
Yet we enslave the Earth.
The Earth is not owned
And neither are our hopes and dreams!

Ethan Rowe (11)
Tamworth Enterprise College, Belgrave

Poaching And Hunting

Let's stop for a second,
Let's think about what we are doing,
Killing the ecosystem.
Let's think for a second about what we're doing.

People poaching and hunting for fun,
We'll die faster,
Just think about the animals,
How do they feel?
Are we killing them for survival?
Really, we are killing species.

If we kill the animals
We will die quicker,
We need animals to live,
Like bees pollinating the crops,
Cows giving us our dairy.

We treat them like objects,
Never giving them respect,
We act like we are the boss,
Putting them in cages,
When all they want is freedom.

Elephants are being killed
Just for their tusks,
Stop for a second and think,
How do animals feel?

Skye Ward (11)
Tamworth Enterprise College, Belgrave

Why Me?

Why me?
Why do I have to be in pain?

I laid in a hard old bed
As the doctor said:
"She'll need surgery."
My stomach twisted in fear
As I shed a tear.

In pain,
I tried to wake myself from the nightmare.
A shock of fear dashed down my body.
Why me?
Seven billion people,
One sick kid.
Me.

One last question as I got wheeled into the operating room.
I thought it was my doom.
Why me?

A beam of light shone into my tired eyes...
I'd made it!
My mum held my hand,
My eyes fully opened,
My mum held me tight,
My heart felt light.

Then I heard the news:

"You can go home soon!"
My face glowed up,
Then I hugged my mum.
I couldn't believe I was leaving,
Then I saw the 'food'.
"Eat it all up!" they said.
Then I squirmed.

Why me?

Evie Alice Ames (11)
Tamworth Enterprise College, Belgrave

Rain And Thunder

Love,
For some, it's sunshine and rainbows,
For others, it's rain and thunder.
Thunder can injure,
Thunder can leave scars.

Thunder,
It comes crashing down,
Then it's gone,
Then it's back.
That unforgettable bang ringing in your ears,
You can never forget the sound of thunder.
Thunder is unforgettable,
Thunder can change you.

Rain,
It can drown you,
It can wash you out,
It can wash away your barrier,
It can flood.
Rain can ruin you,
Rain can change you.

Rain and thunder,
Definitely not the same as sunshine and rainbows.
Instead of colour,
It's just black and white,
No real colour.

Just greys mixing with whites.

Rain and thunder drain you.
Rain and thunder change you.

Hollie Dixon (15)
Tamworth Enterprise College, Belgrave

Dogs

I was in the shop
Then I heard a pop
The bell rang
The birds all sang

I heard squeaking
But I was weakening
I was nervous
Also, curious

I saw them
Then showed my jaw to them
It isn't *our* fault
We're dogs

They petted us
And then...
We were bought!
Only two

We looked identical
That was why
Oh wow
£1,000?

Oh jeez
One had to go...
It was me!

There was one that shone
She was the only one
She was beautiful
I was 'cute'

Many looked like me
Like we were identical
I felt dead, it had led
To only us two...

I wasn't actually dead
But I felt dead inside!
I trusted them more
More than I thought.

Imogen Daws (11)
Tamworth Enterprise College, Belgrave

Puzzles

I am special
I am different
I am a puzzle
I am me

I'm a puzzle piece
I'm unique
Everyone who is like me
Is slightly different

I hear voices everywhere
I wonder if they are really there
I see colours really bright
My mind is full of surprises

I see you looking at me
I see you judging me
I see you thinking that I'm weird.
Yes,
I have Autism

The world would be boring
If we were all the same
Different makes life interesting
My life is different
No two days are the same

Do I wish I was normal?
Sometimes

But Autism is a part of me
And that will never change

It is who I am
It defines me
It makes me special
It makes me different!

Alexandra Leskiewicz (12)
Tamworth Enterprise College, Belgrave

Her Final Breath

She always wore a smile,
However, that only lasted for a while.
It felt as though her heart had been torn
Over and over, just like before.

Memories lingering in her mind,
She just wanted men to be kind.
The emptiness stayed inside,
This began to lead up to the day she died.

Carrying on the constant battle with herself,
She prayed for her final breath.
She changed her path,
Now people began to stare and laugh.

She wasn't even close with anyone anymore,
Even lonelier than before.
Tears no longer poured down her face
As she ran her final race.

It has now come to an end,
She was her only friend.
No one was left by her side,
28th of July is the day she died.

Kara Thompson (14)
Tamworth Enterprise College, Belgrave

WWII Prisoners

Spent my whole life in a cell
Didn't even go to school to learn how to spell.
Thrown on the floor, gun to the head
Move and already I'm dead.
Every night I cry
When I see other kids, I sigh
I arrived to die
It's either good morning or goodbye.

I once was free to roam
But now I want to return home.
I hear all the bombs and screams
I don't have nice dreams.
I have no one to trust
I will fight back if I must.

Children sat on brick
In the middle of deserted sticks.
When will this war end?
Peace is what I want to send.
What if all my friends die?
I just want to cry.
I am just a child
It's been years since I last smiled.

Aidan Matthew Whetton (14)
Tamworth Enterprise College, Belgrave

Little Do They Know

You have one chance,
Impress them,
You try to be perfect.
But little do they know
The stress at home,
Just to look perfect.

Bullying is a disease,
It is as contagious as flu.
It infects the mind,
Like brain cancer,
Little do they know
That brain cancer kills.

Truth be told,
We are judged.
Every action,
Every word,
Every time they win.

Little do they know,
We victims are like an ocean,
Growing every day.
Little do they know
They affect our mental health,
Anxiety rises every day.

Many do know,
Plenty do know,
They're slowly killing us,
One by one...

Little do they know
Water overpowers flames.
Little do they know,
We've won.

Laura Jade McKeown (12)
Tamworth Enterprise College, Belgrave

The Future

The future is a place of hope,
For the planet, the people and their civilisations.
But the impact of the past
Can affect the future!

Your GCSEs, jobs and futures are taught at school,
But maybe not enough.
Skills range far and wide
But you might not have planned enough time.
Houses you like, you may not buy
But at least you're happy.

Say if you're naughty, or not at all,
Your future might be affected, or not at all.
Your future is in your hands
As long as you follow it as you planned.
But if you're naughty all the time
You might not follow your plan at all.
Just remember, you're as perfect as can be.
The future is in *your* hands.

Leland Cooper (12)
Tamworth Enterprise College, Belgrave

Living With Animals

Every day is a great pleasure,
Spending every hour, all of us together,
It's better than finding buried treasure,
I could live this life forever.

There's no better life than living at the zoo,
So many animals to see,
There's always something to do,
Apart from the summer when I'm chased by the buzzing bee!

It's fun to feed the animals at the zoo,
Lions, tigers and reptiles all for you,
Even though I have to clean the poo,
Bright and early in the morning dew.

Looking after the babies is hard enough,
Because they always wind you up,
But you still have the teenagers acting all tough,
Monkeys swinging their arms around, throwing the cups!

Maison Biddle (11)
Tamworth Enterprise College, Belgrave

Shocking, Scary Social Media

Every time another joins,
Another danger strikes,
Everyone building their coins,
Waiting patiently for more likes,
Thousands of streaks,
Finally uploaded,
More and more gossip leaks,
It's nearly loaded,
Photos and photos covered in filters,
Just press share,
Some of the rumours hurt more than splinters,
In a world of media, it's just not fair,
Seconds on your story,
Most of this happens online,
Most in this world is often gory,
Whose life is it affecting? Mine.
Making a new blog,
Opening lines,
It's as if you can't see through the fog.
When nobody sees it, then
Boom!
Someone will find out soon.

Summer Mae McLaren (11)
Tamworth Enterprise College, Belgrave

Death Row

Here I am,
Sitting at death row,
Goodbye to my family,
Goodbye to my foes.

I'm suffering from this pain,
I'm not the one to blame,
Pleading for my innocence,
The answer never changed.

Locked up in a cell,
Would rather be in Hell,
I should not be here,
I should be treated well.

But what have I done?
My time has come,
My future is done,
Am I just here for them to have fun?

Wrong place, wrong time,
I didn't commit the crime,
Now I'm chained up.
I'm all ready to die,
I've had my last meal,
Chicken with thyme,
This has been fun but I'm done with this rhyme...

Logan Darson Bennett (12)
Tamworth Enterprise College, Belgrave

Bad Vs Good

I am a failure,
Don't try to convince me that
I can do it if I try,
My body will break down.
I refuse to believe
That I can do it,
They're better off without me,
You'll never hear me say
"I am worth fighting for."
I am a disappointment.
Don't try to convince me that
I am a champion.

I am a champion,
Don't try to convince me that
I am a disappointment.
I am worth fighting for,
You'll never hear me say,
"They're better off without me."
I can do it,
I refuse to believe that
My body will break down.
I can do it if I try,
Don't try to convince me that
I am a failure.

Stacy Stroud (11)
Tamworth Enterprise College, Belgrave

Celebrity

C elebrities are people living their lives, their futures, and only some lucky people get noticed.

E veryone looks up to them and they inspire most of the world.

L ove is given so much to these amazing celebrities who change people's lives.

E very place they go, like a concert, more inspiration they give to the world.

"B e yourself," they say, but the only thing we want is to be them.

R espect and love we show them.

I nspired people following their dreams and letting nothing get in their way.

T ruthful celebs sharing their news with the world.

Y ou follow your dreams and let your dreams take you through life!

Jessica Jones (11)
Tamworth Enterprise College, Belgrave

The Future

Smoke in the air,
Plastic in the sea,
Don't kill the Earth,
Because then it will just be you
And you won't want that,
Will you?

Children, they are the future,
Don't bully them,
Treat them well,
You were one of them
And you wouldn't want that
To happen to you.

Some animals are endangered,
We need to stop killing
Or there will be no more.
Who cares about meat?
Who cares about tusks?
Who cares if it's fun?
They are living,
Well, *were*.

Don't destroy habitats,
It's like destroying homes,
Do we need as much wood?
Do we need as much metal?
We need to stop.

Luca Sidoli (11)
Tamworth Enterprise College, Belgrave

Jolly Old Man

I knew a place where I would always be
Made to feel safe and happy
Where a jolly old man with a tooth of gold
Would dispense wisdom because he was very old
He would tell me of times way back
When his hair wasn't short and grey but curly and black
He would listen to my problems
God knows how I love this bloke
He would chase away my sadness with a single joke.

Maybe I didn't cherish my time as I oughta
Grandad, how I loved being your granddaughter.

When my kids have kids I'll try to be
Exactly what you were to me
As they get older and continue to grow
I endeavour to be their hero.

Emma Greenway (12)
Tamworth Enterprise College, Belgrave

Emergency Services

E mergency!
M illions of calls come in per day
E very day is a mystery
R ushing around all day, every day
G etting into uniform
E ntering the danger zone
N ot scared of anything
C arrying people to safety
Y elling at people to evacuate

S aving millions of lives
E vacuating from buildings
R ushing to save lives
V ehicles pulling up to the emergency
I n a rush to save lives
C arrying equipment as they enter the fire
E vacuating the scene as everyone's safe
S aving their lives always.

Shaun David Dunham (12)
Tamworth Enterprise College, Belgrave

Broken

In my own jail of thoughts,
I work my life away
To see the overgrowing courts,
After everyone goes, I just lay

Waiting for all the pain
To disappear after all,
I always stay in my lane,
They all surround me, ever so tall.

They see fear
Always in my eyes,
I quietly drink beer,
Every second, a part of me dies.

Every day I just wait
Patiently for my time to go,
My life is just a sad fate
As my body is reaching ever so low.

As I lay on the floor,
All around me is red,
I could hear a great war
As I went to bed.

Finally, I can rest...

Ellie-Mae Williams-Moore (11)
Tamworth Enterprise College, Belgrave

Parents Make You Strong

Parents carry your weight on their shoulders
Until you get older.
They teach you right or wrong through the days
And it makes you learn in many ways.
Many people can judge you
But your parents are there to get you through.
Throughout your life, your parents are your role models,
They taught you first to waddle.
Now, when you're older,
Your memories get bolder.
You start to choose how to live your life,
Even the time when you will get a wife.
It's time to get a job,
You could make a film like 'The Blob'.
Or you could fight in the war,
Or play football and cause a draw.

Oliver Smallwood (11)
Tamworth Enterprise College, Belgrave

Past

The future, no one knows
What it has in store...
Flying cars or cars without wheels?
Your future is up to you
And only you can control the way you choose to go.

The past happened and nobody knows your home life.
People try to be brave, but there's a time everyone cries.
Your past doesn't have to be a problem
And no need to keep it to yourself.
Be heard and do not fear.

The past has memories you will constantly have in your head.
In the future, you are the driver
Time to steer your own future.

Be brave
Because the past is nothing to be afraid of.

Oliver Deakin
Tamworth Enterprise College, Belgrave

My Heroes Are My Family

My heroes are my beautiful family
They are loud
They are strong
They are lovely
We are argumentative
But they make me happy when I am sad.
My heroes are my beautiful family.

My heroes are my beautiful family
They are loud
They are strong
They are lovely
We watch films together
We have days out together
My family are the best
No one can replace my family.

My heroes are my beautiful family
They are loud
They are strong
They are lovely
We are argumentative
But they make me happy when I am sad.
My heroes are my beautiful family.

Stella-Faith Powell (14)
Tamworth Enterprise College, Belgrave

Being Me!

I might think differently to others
I may look differently to others
But when did that stop me?

I am not that pretty girl that sits next to me in English!
But I am my own person
With my own choices.

Trust me when I say this depression is not a choice
I did not wake up one day and decide to be depressed.
No!
That is not how it works.

I look back when the road says forward
I should only look forward
Never go back...

Depression has its own words
Just like I do.

Just speak louder than depression.
I'm me; not anyone else!

Lacey Louise Wayne (11)
Tamworth Enterprise College, Belgrave

Social Media

Snapchat streaks,
Photos getting leaked,
People stalking on the map,
Hoping not to get hacked!

Liking this, liking that,
Photos are being looked at.
People following what you do,
Everything online may not always be true.

Never always accept what you see,
To see a whole video or photo, it can sometimes never be,
No one is perfect, whatever we post,
Who cares about the likes and who has the most?

Facebook, WhatsApp, Instagram and Snapchat
Are all really the same,
Posting pics about your life,
They all just have a different name.

Tia Williams (11)
Tamworth Enterprise College, Belgrave

Pets Alone

Roses are red, violets are blue,
Animal abuse is bad and it's caused by you.
Animal abuse is the worst,
Anyone who does it should be cursed.
I hate seeing pets without an owner,
Whoever abandons them becomes a loner.
Reckless ownership is really crummy,
Keep your pets or you're a dummy.
Bunnies that hop around all day,
In the shade is where they would lay.
Stalking their prey,
They will pounce at the stroke of day.

Keep and protect your pets till death do you part,
And when they die, you can then let down your guard.

Michael Reeves (12)
Tamworth Enterprise College, Belgrave

Love Or Hate Against The Queen

As days go by,
Nights pass too,
The Queen does work
We don't know about.

People say, "The Queen is terrible!"
"The Queen doesn't do anything!"
"The Queen doesn't give to the homeless!"
"She only goes to weddings and world leader meetings!"

But she's polite to anyone she meets,
She would never hurt anyone,
Her children and grandchildren adore her,
She pleases everyone she meets.

"She doesn't help us!"
"She's lazy for a queen!"
Just ignore what they say,
The Queen is amazing!
She helps everyone she can!

Amelia Powell (11)
Tamworth Enterprise College, Belgrave

Think Of Love

We're in a war
I'm thinking of love
Friends and family
Lives on your shoulders

So we should think of your life after the war
So many smiling faces
So many proud parents
So think about your life after the war

We're in the trenches
We're losing, but
We can make a comeback
And protect our country.

So think about the future
Children play
Parents watching
Everyone is happy.

So see you on the other side
Comrade and captain
See you later...
I've got a war to fight.

Jake Inscoe (12)
Tamworth Enterprise College, Belgrave

Meningitis

Where am I?
What year is it?
The doctor said 1994.
"You have been in a coma for four weeks."
What day is it?
"It is 14th March 1994."
Who am I?
"You are Lee Paul Taylor, born 21st September 1979."

What is it?
Why is it a thing?
It's a killer
It has hit thousands of people
My dad has been hit by this creature
This disease
Every step he takes he remembers those weeks in a coma
When I see him, I get emotional
My dad's dreams were crushed
He wanted to be a Royal Marine.

Charlie Arthur Taylor (11)
Tamworth Enterprise College, Belgrave

Circle Of Crime

Dreams have been crushed,
Souls have been hurt,
Darkness has been spread.
This has all happened
Because of you.
You have killed
Thousands of people.
You've done this
Only you.

Gunshots haunt my dreams
Like I could feel most of it.

Blood is everywhere,
The Reaper is coming,
There is nothing
You can do,
We are all
Going to die!

Mountains of guilt
Spread around us,
Piles of bones
Fall on top of us
Like I am seconds
Away from death...

Rivith Weligama Palliyaguruge (11)
Tamworth Enterprise College, Belgrave

Lego Obama Yoda

President I am,
Best friends I am with Sam,
The children in my basement
Are filled with excitement.

I was just a young green boy,
Fiddling with my nan's toy,
Then the president found me
And enslaved my family,
My nan died,
I really cried,
I am Lego Obama Yoda.

Being President is hard,
My big toe is very charred,
I let the kids escape,
I now wear a cape,
I met a man called Andy.
He stole all the candy,
He looked like cupid,
He was very stupid!

Flynn Francis (11)
Tamworth Enterprise College, Belgrave

War Zone

If I die in a war zone,
Box me up and send me home.

Put my medals on my chest,
Tell my mom I did my best.

Tell my dad not to bow,
He won't get tension from me now.

Tell my bro to study perfectly,
The key of my bike will be his permanently.

Tell my sister not to be upset,
Her bro will take a long sleep after sunset.

Tell my nation not to cry,
Because I'm a soldier born to die.

Alaric James Johnson (11)
Tamworth Enterprise College, Belgrave

Harry Potter

H arry is a wizard
A t Hogwarts
R uns away and never comes back
R uns back to where he came from
Y esterday, he was practising more magic with Hermione

P rofessor Dumbledore introduced Harry
O n the ocean boat
T ime to sail back to Hogwarts
T o walk up the stairs
E ach of us all standing in the hall
R eady to be put in houses.

Max David Wiseman (15)
Tamworth Enterprise College, Belgrave

Death Row

Living a death sentence,
Held in a prison,
Trapped on death row,
A row full of pain,
A row full of depression,
Imprisoned within a body,
Locked in tight,
Just take that final walk.

Take those final pain-filled steps,
Walk down death row,
It would all just end,
All the pain,
All those haunting thoughts,
It would all just end,
It would all just go away,
But instead...

McKenzie Lowe (14)
Tamworth Enterprise College, Belgrave

No Chicken

KFC fries like...
They have been outside in the rain.
As if they've soaked up all the oil.
As if they're made of bread fished from the pond.

Ran out of chicken...
What happens if KFC runs out of chicken?
Will it be FC (fried chips) for the night?
What is like with no chicken?
It's just a chippy.
What happens when there's no chicken?
What is it like, KFC?

Jack Stephen Mott (12)
Tamworth Enterprise College, Belgrave

Queen

Q ueen: royal, rich but could do a little more for the world.

U nderstood that she basically owns the UK, doesn't mean she can act like she rules the whole universe.

E verybody makes sure they look smart for respect when they see her in a car, roaming around the streets of London.

E verybody should obey the law but some don't.

N ever forget she has the cutest Corgis!

Lily-May Deakin (12)
Tamworth Enterprise College, Belgrave

A Poem About Kylian Mbappé

Mbappé is my favourite footballer,
I want to be as fast as him when I'm a baller,
As he puts defenders in their shame,
He's the youngest player with so much fame,
He's obviously the fastest player,
While he blasts it past David de Gea,
He plays for the team PSG,
He's better than Messi,
Mbappé is my favourite footballer.

James Malin (11)
Tamworth Enterprise College, Belgrave

Education

E xciting lessons to learn new stuff.

D isastrous homework!

U nderstanding the meaning of verbs.

C ool experiments in science.

A mazing PE lessons.

T hinking of finishing and starting school.

I 've wasted time learning!

O ur lives wasted by six hours.

N ew learning with every lesson.

Owen Mudie (11)

Tamworth Enterprise College, Belgrave

Death Row

Death row is horrible,
It is a punishment,
People should be put on death row,
Some humans are horrible,
Humans should die for fatal crimes,
Murders, psychopaths, cold-blooded killers,
Making families grieve when they shouldn't,
Parents losing sons and daughters,
Innocent people dying,
Death row is
Deserved.

Sharissa Morgan Monks (11)
Tamworth Enterprise College, Belgrave

Politician Love Or Hate

Some people think Boris Johnson and Donald Trump are
idiots,
And I agree.

For a start, Boris Johnson wants to deliver Brexit on the 31st
of October,
And he has locked down Parliament for God knows how
long.

Donald Trump has access to all the government
And nearly the world
And he wants to destroy the world...

Aimee-Louise Angela Tunnicliffe (11)
Tamworth Enterprise College, Belgrave

Banksy!

Would you like to spend your life on the streets,
Or do you want to spend your life eating expensive sweets?
Then value your life,
Work hard for your wife.
There are people out there like Banksy who enjoy their life.
Try and push yourself to be like them.
If you do, then...
You will go far!

Addison Lake (11)
Tamworth Enterprise College, Belgrave

Like Boys, Like Girls

Like boys, like girls,
We are like pearls
That should shine out to the world,
No matter what they say,
We should always stay,
Stand with us on the rainbow,
Don't let the rain knock us off,
Don't let the thunder break us down,
Stand with us
On the rainbow.

Madison Mae Bounds (12)
Tamworth Enterprise College, Belgrave

For The Man

For the man who is selfish,
For the man who is the president of America,
For the man who has assisted in nuclear bombs,
For the man who is an idiot,
For the man who is a stupid orange!

If you haven't guessed,
It is Donald Trump!

Ronnie Jay Mossop (11)
Tamworth Enterprise College, Belgrave

The Bad Side Of Social Media

It was all okay,
I was happy.
I had a great life,
But it all changed.

I downloaded this app
And I added people I didn't know.
They started to talk to me:
"Hi ugly."
"Eww."
I was in shock.

Amelia Coggan (11)
Tamworth Enterprise College, Belgrave

A Girl's Life

I'm not the prettiest girl,
But I'm not the ugliest girl,
I'm moody and moany,
I'm grumpy and groany,
My smile isn't the brightest,
But my cry isn't the darkest,
I'm not the dumbest girl,
But I'm not the smartest girl.

Maisie Root (12)
Tamworth Enterprise College, Belgrave

NHS Staff

N ight shifts
H eightened emotions
S taff running around

S afeguarding patients
T hreats to staff
A ssaults
F rightened
F ailure to provide the care they want to give.

Callum Johnson (12)

Tamworth Enterprise College, Belgrave

Living With Shadows

The hinges creak open
His feet dragging against the floor
In his hand, a weapon
The weapon that could destroy all of humanity
On the side of the bottle
The words read: 'Alcohol, please drink responsibly'...

Bradley Rylatt (12)
Tamworth Enterprise College, Belgrave